Wildlife in Danger

Chatham Island forget-me-not

monkey-eating eagle

hawksbill turtle

Javan rhinoceros

Queen Alexandra's birdwing

The publishers would like to thank the staff of World Wildlife Fund for their help in making these books.

LADYBIRD BOOKS, INC.
Auburn, Maine 04210 U.S.A.
© LADYBIRD BOOKS LTD 1989
Loughborough, Leicestershire, England
Panda logo © 1986 Copyright WWF – International

Printed in England

WORLD WILDLIFE FUND

Our World in Danger

written by GILLIAN DORFMAN
illustrated by TONY MORRIS and CHRIS REED

Ladybird Books

Produced in association with World Wildlife Fund

People are animals.
They are alive. They eat,
breathe, move, and have
babies — just like other
animals.

But in many ways people
are different from other
animals.

We think in a different way. And we do things to the Earth that can change our lives and the lives of animals and plants that share our world.

We cut down forests to make room for roads, dams, farms, and towns.

When we do this we kill many beautiful and useful plants, and we destroy the homes of wild animals.

A hummingbird sips nectar from a flower.

Beautiful orchids grow high in the trees.

A jaguar hides among the leaves, waiting to surprise its prey.

We build houses, factories, and stores. We build highways, railroads, airports, schools, and hospitals.

We can change the land to build on it. But often, changing the land destroys the homes of wild animals. If an animal loses its home, it may die.

This avocet builds its nest in wetlands. Many wetlands are disappearing because we are draining them to use the land for building or farming.

We grow crops and raise animals for food. But people do not always farm wisely.

Many farmers spray their fields with chemicals. Some chemicals help the crops grow strong and healthy. Other chemicals kill weeds and pests.

But people often use chemicals without thinking about the harm they can do to other living things.

These fish were killed by chemicals that rain washed off farmland and into the river.

Many peregrine falcons have been poisoned by chemicals sprayed on crops. The chemicals kill the birds or stop them from rearing young.

In some places people try to raise too many animals on poor land.

The herds eat up all the plants.

There are not enough plants to keep the soil in place. So when the wind blows, and the rain falls, the soil is carried away.

The land becomes bare.
Nothing can live or grow on it.

Often, we do not think carefully enough about what we are doing, or the damage we are doing to our world.

We dump garbage on the land.

Fumes from cars, factories, and power stations pollute the air we breathe.

We pollute rivers and seas where fish and other creatures live.

Sometimes oil tankers spill oil at sea, killing birds and other sea life. The oil then washes ashore, harming wildlife along the coasts and spoiling the beaches.

Some beautiful animals are killed so that people can have expensive clothes and jewelry to wear or unusual ornaments for their homes.

Wild cats like this leopard are killed for their skins, which are made into fur coats.

Many elephants are killed for their tusks. The tusks are made of ivory, which is carved into ornaments and jewelry.

Crocodile skins are made into shoes, handbags, and belts.

Rare plants and animals are taken from the wild and sold to people in other countries far away.

There are laws to stop people from buying and selling rare wildlife. Yet the buying and selling still goes on, because smugglers get high prices for these goods, and make lots of money.

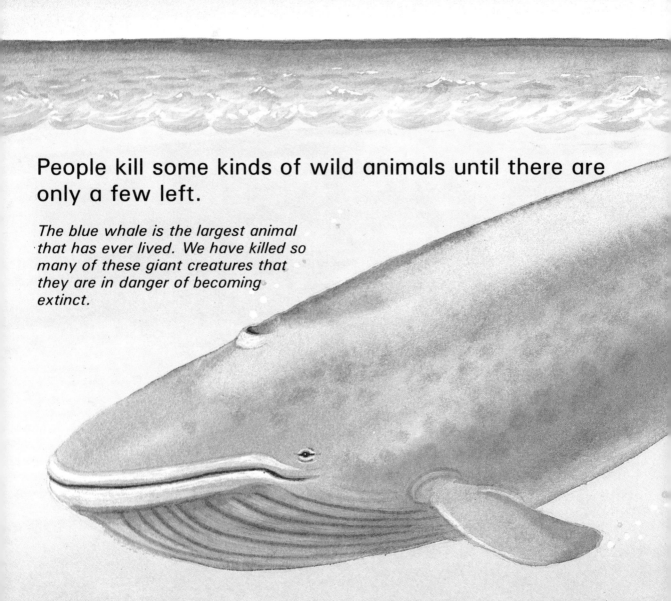

People kill some kinds of wild animals until there are only a few left.

The blue whale is the largest animal that has ever lived. We have killed so many of these giant creatures that they are in danger of becoming extinct.

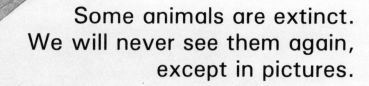

Some animals are extinct.
We will never see them again,
except in pictures.

Dodos once lived on an island called Mauritius, where they had no enemies.
Then people arrived, bringing rats and pet dogs with them.
The dogs and rats killed the dodos. Today there are none left.

Very often it is people who harm nature. So we are the ones who must think of ways to care for our world.

One way is to set aside special places where wild animals and plants can live safely.

We have many national parks where animals like the bison and coyote are protected.

We must learn to live *with* nature, and not destroy it.

In many dry lands there are very few trees. The number is getting smaller as people chop the trees down and use the wood for cooking, keeping warm, and building homes.

But people can
plant more trees...

...use stoves that don't
burn much wood...

...and build their
homes from other
materials, instead
of wood.

Some people are trying to save wild animals that are in danger of being lost forever.

These scientists study the giant panda and the way it lives. With this knowledge, people may be able to protect this animal and its home.

Many more wild plants and animals still need to be saved.

American alligator

tiger

Arabian oryx

You can help protect the world's wildlife. Don't buy plants and animals that have been taken illegally from the wild.

No rare animals sold here

Look at wild plants and animals without disturbing them.

You will be helping to make our world a better place to live.

Glossary

extinct   Animals or plants that have died out.

national park   An area that is protected because it is the home of important or rare plants and animals.

pests   Animals that cause problems for people by eating crops or spreading disease.

pollute   To spoil or harm the natural world.

weeds   Wild plants that grow where they are not wanted.

wetlands   Areas where land and water meet, such as marshes, swamps, lakes, and ponds.

Acknowledgments:
The publishers would like to thank the following for permission to reproduce photographs:
J. Allan Cash p. 16 top right; Ardea p. 7 top left (W. Weisser), top right (A. Warren),
p. 16 top left (J. Van Gruisen), bottom (I. Beames), p. 25 top left (C. McDougal), top right
(P. Morris), bottom (J. Swedberg), back cover (P. Morris); Tim Clark p. 5 left, p. 11 left;
The Hutchison Library p. 4 left and right, p. 5 right; WWF p. 7 bottom (Y. J. Rey-Millet),
p. 9 (H. Ausloos), p. 11 right (U. Häyrinen), p. 15 (J. M. Baker), p. 23 top left (M. Erbetta),
top right (Bellerive Foundation), bottom (J. Newby).